charms

by Sophie Robertson

THE GUILD OF MASTER CRAFTSMAN
PUBLICATIONS

First published 2013 by
Guild of Master Craftsman Publications Ltd
Castle Place, 166 High Street, Lewes,
East Sussex BN7 1XU

Publisher Jonathan Bailey
Production Manager Jim Bulley
Managing Editor Gerrie Purcell
Senior Project Editor Dominique Page
Editor Judith Chamberlain-Webber
Managing Art Editor Gilda Pacitti
Designer Rob Janes
Photographer Andrew Perris

Set in King and Myriad
Colour origination by GMC Reprographics
Printed and bound in China

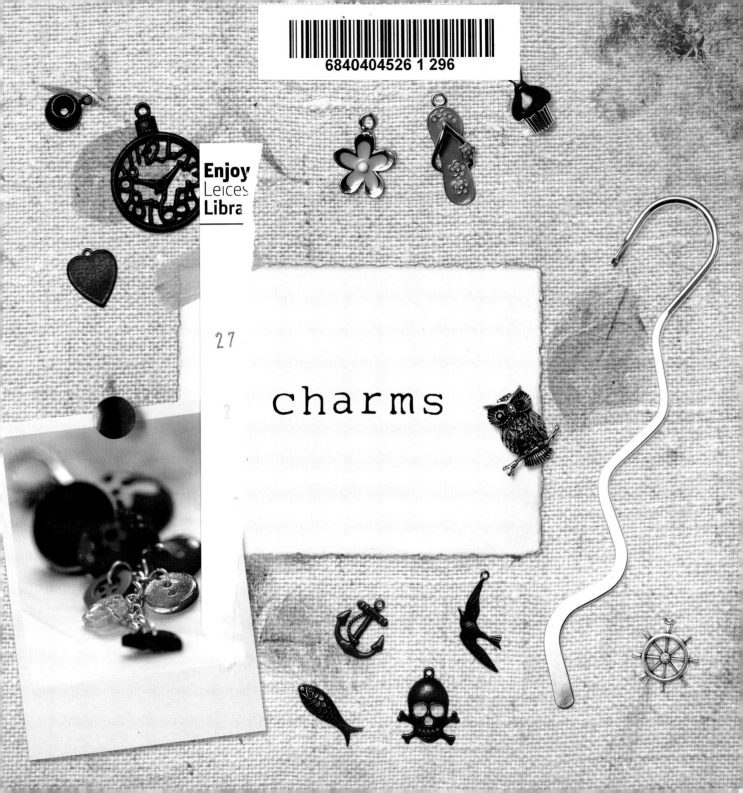

charms

contents

Tools and Materials

Basic Techniques

Continued...

NATASHA

CARA

FIESTA

DREAMCATCHER

NAUTICAL

LADYBIRD

AMY

FLUTTER

The Projects

OWL

CANARY

BUTTON

ROXY

PEARL

ROBYN

SWEETHEART

POLLY

CLOVER

CRYSTAL

ALICE

ANNA

Tools and Materials

THE FOLLOWING PAGES WILL SHOW YOU THE MOST COMMONLY USED TOOLS THAT WILL HELP YOU TO CREATE YOUR CHARM PROJECTS AND WILL EXPLAIN WHAT TYPES OF MATERIALS YOU SHOULD LOOK FOR.

pliers

Pliers are possibly the most important tools used in jewellery making and craft projects. They are used for holding, opening and closing, shaping and forming wire and components; there are different types available for specific jobs. Don't worry if you only have a couple of types – you will still be able to get most jobs done!

FLAT-NOSE PLIERS

These have flat parallel jaws that don't taper. They are useful for bending and flattening wire, squeezing ribbon crimps and also holding, opening and closing jump rings and other findings.

ROUND-NOSE PLIERS

These have completely round jaws that taper to a point at the end. They are used for making eyepins and bending wire into loops, coils and spirals.

SNIPE-NOSE PLIERS

With half-round jaws on the outside, flat parallel faces on the inside and tapering from a wider base to smaller tip, these are also sometimes called chain-nose pliers. Their small tip makes them very useful for holding, and opening and closing small components and jump rings.

MULTI-SIZED LOOPING PLIERS

This pair of pliers has three different sizes of completely round, non-tapered jaws. By wrapping wire around the jaws you can make jump rings and loops of different sizes.

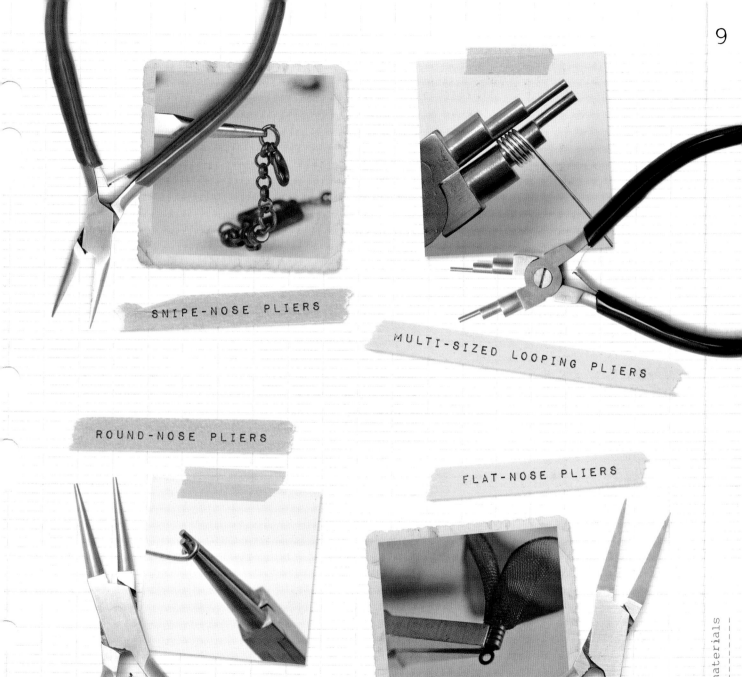

SNIPE-NOSE PLIERS

MULTI-SIZED LOOPING PLIERS

ROUND-NOSE PLIERS

FLAT-NOSE PLIERS

Tools and materials

cutters

Cutters are another essential tool when working with wire and there are several types to choose from depending on your needs. Do not use these cutters on steel memory wire, as they are suitable for soft wires only and the sharp cutting edge will be damaged.

END CUTTERS

The cutter is at the end of this tool and is suitable for cutting thin materials, chain and wire. The design of this tool lets you get right up close to your design to snip off any excess wire and leave you with a flush finish.

SIDE CUTTERS

Similar to end cutters, but the cutter runs along the side of these. Use the flat side against the end of the wire you are keeping, as it will leave you with a neater cut edge. The tips are handy for getting into small spaces such as individual links of small chain.

METAL SNIPS

Straight-sided shears, like scissors for metal, these are suitable for cutting small areas of sheet metal and very fine wire. They are also useful for trimming leather and ribbon.

FABRIC SCISSORS

These specialist scissors with extremely sharp blades are designed for cutting fabric. Do not cut anything other than fabric with them, as this will blunt the blades.

EMBROIDERY SCISSORS

Small scissors with sharp tips, these can trim threads neatly and accurately.

END CUTTERS

FABRIC SCISSORS

EMBROIDERY SCISSORS

METAL SNIPS

SIDE CUTTERS

Tools and materials

miscellaneous

These are non-specialist items that are widely available from DIY and craft shops, and are needed for certain jobs in many of the projects.

ADHESIVE

Non-toxic, multi-purpose PVA glue bonds wood, ceramics, felt, fabric, leather, glass and more, and so is ideal for use with most craft projects.

A dot of superglue is perfect for securing knots in thread, cord or elastic and is extremely quick setting. Epoxy resin is a stronger adhesive that is suitable for gluing pearls or beads to metal findings.

TAPE MEASURE

This is an extremely important tool for measuring the correct amount of chain, cord, ribbon and so on that is needed for your design.

EMERY PAPER

This can be used to soften any sharp edges on pieces of wire, especially if they are to be used to make jewellery findings.

ADHESIVE

EMERY PAPER

LIGHTER

This can be used to carefully melt the ends of threads or ribbons slightly to prevent them from fraying. Hold the lighter to them for a fraction of a second only.

STRING

This is useful for finding the circumference of a wrist or neck, to measure against a ruler, if you don't have a tape measure handy.

LIGHTER

STRING

TAPE MEASURE

KEEP A COLLECTION OF THESE AND ANY OTHER ITEMS YOU FEEL MAY COME IN HANDY. THEY ARE BOUND TO BE USEFUL FOR ALL KINDS OF FUTURE CRAFT PROJECTS.

Tools and materials

materials

Charms are clearly going to be the main focus of the projects in this book, but there are lots of other materials that you will need to use alongside them to create the basis of, or add further interest to, your designs.

CHARMS

There is a huge range of beautiful, quirky or fun charms that are readily available for you to use. In fact, almost anything you can imagine wanting in a miniature version will exist somewhere! Made from cast metal in all sorts of finishes, or glass, plastic, wood, ceramic, polymer clay and Swarovski crystal, they have a loop at the top so that they can be attached to any design using jump rings, bails or eyepins.

In the last few years, a new type of charm called the European charm has become a worldwide, personalized jewellery phenomenon. European charms are charm beads with a large hole through the centre and have either carved, enamelled or painted decoration all the way around the outside; sometimes a further dangling small charm is attached. They can be made from metal, glass or ceramics and thread easily onto bracelets and necklaces. One of the coolest trends is 'upcycling' common objects into wearable accessories. Re-use buttons, toys, sweets or vintage textiles; revitalize old treasures by using broken or unwanted jewellery components to create unique and cost-effective charms; or find natural objects such as shells and feathers that can easily be transformed into beautiful charms for your designs.

CONNECTORS

These are beads or charms with loops on each side, so they can easily be connected to your design or connected to other charms.

CHARMS

CHAIN

Chain is an essential element of many charm designs, because whether you are making a charm bracelet or a key ring, charms can easily be attached to any link of the chain. There are lots of different shapes, sizes and finishes of chain available.

Curb: This has uniformly sized round or oval links but they are twisted so that they interlock when laid flat along a surface. This style of chain is available in a wide variety of widths.

Fancy chain: This is an umbrella term for any decorative or unusual variation of a standard chain type. For example, the fancy curb chain used in this book features two different-sized, thinner-than-usual links.

Trace: This is generally a simple, fine and delicate chain, which typically has oval links that are uniform in breadth and thickness.

You will need to buy the chain unfinished; i.e., without any catches already attached. Alternatively, you can create your own unique chain, using what are known as 'Quick Links' and connectors that come in a huge choice of shapes and sizes.

CONNECTORS

CURB

FANCY CHAIN

TRACE

BEADS

There are a huge amount of beads available in many colours, shapes, sizes, materials and prices. They can add interest and colour to your designs, act as spacers between charms or form a unique design on which to attach your charms.

SUEDE / LEATHER / WAXED CORD

All of these cords or thongs are usually sold by the metre and are used to create friendship-style bracelets and necklaces. Charms and beads can easily be threaded onto single strands or, if multiple cords are plaited together, charms can be attached using jump rings.

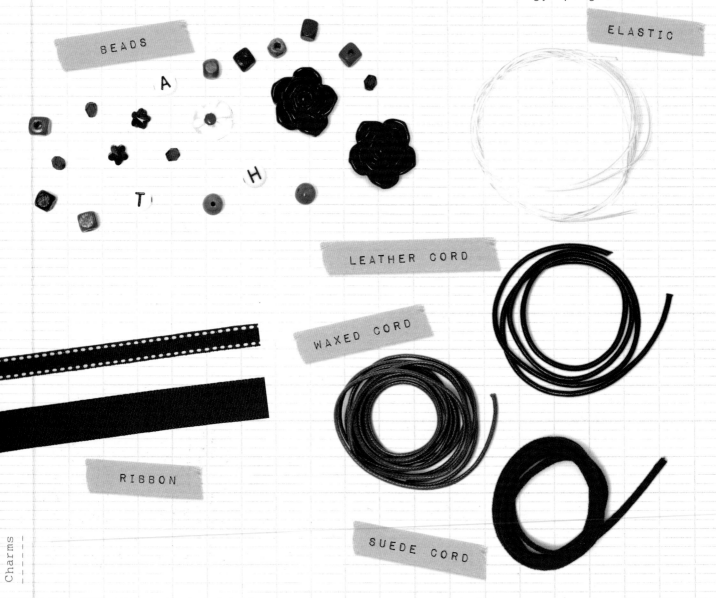

BEADS

ELASTIC

LEATHER CORD

WAXED CORD

RIBBON

SUEDE CORD

RIBBON

Ribbon comes in many different materials, including satin, velvet and silk, and is available in all colours, designs and widths. It can be used for decoration but is also great for using in place of, or alongside, chain to create necklaces and bracelets. For strength and rigidity, I recommend grosgrain ribbon, which is woven, has a ribbed appearance and tends to feel thicker than most ribbons.

ELASTIC

You can thread beads and charms onto clear or coloured elastic thread to create gorgeous bracelets and necklaces that stretch and slide on and off easily.

LEATHER / FELT / PATTERNED TEXTILES

Use fancy fabric to cover beads and buttons or create whole charm designs with leather or felt. You can always find cheap offcuts of leather in fabric and craft stores or you can scour charity shops and recycle old textiles.

LEATHER

FELT

PATTERNED TEXTILES

findings

Findings are all the little components used in jewellery making, and other crafts, that serve a mechanical function, such as attaching, joining or linking parts together. There are lots of ready-made findings available in various finishes to buy, but you can also make some of them yourself if you need something unique for your design (see pages 21–4).

EARRINGS

You can use simple earring hooks with a decorative coil and ball, and an open loop at the bottom, to hang charms, chain or beads from. Alternatively, a classic ball stud on a straight post with an open loop underneath allows you to attach charms, chain or beads to create stunning drop earrings.

RIBBON/CORD CRIMPS

These are available in various different sizes and shapes to match the width of the ribbon, cord, leather thong or feather that you want to attach it to. When closed with pliers, they securely grasp the end of the material and have a loop attached so you can easily connect them to your design.

JUMP RINGS

A jump ring is a single loop of wire that can be any size or thickness and is used to connect findings and jewellery together or to join or attach charms.

TRIGGER/LOBSTER CATCHES

A clasp commonly used opposite a jump ring to fasten necklaces and bracelets, the catch is opened by pulling back the tiny trigger to move the piece of metal covering the opening – and of course it closes when released!

T-BAR AND LOOP FITTINGS

The T-bar is a type of fastener. It is a straight bar, with a loop halfway along the underside for a jump ring to attach to the end of a chain. The loop is attached to the other end of the chain and is large enough for the T-bar to pass through but not to fall back out.

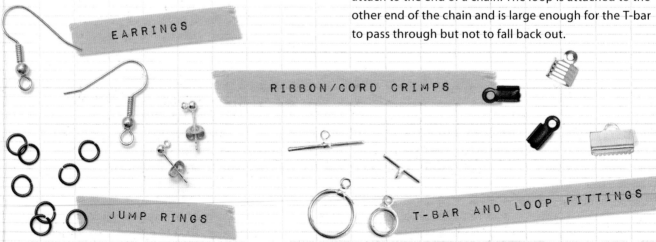

EARRINGS

RIBBON/CORD CRIMPS

JUMP RINGS

T-BAR AND LOOP FITTINGS

SPLIT RINGS FOR KEY RINGS

These are double rings, open at both ends, which are strong enough for keys to be threaded onto. Attach a large jump ring with a piece of chain around large rings so that you can add charms and beads.

MOBILE PHONE LARIAT

This looped cord has a large jump ring attached to the bottom, ready for you to decorate with beads and charms. Simply thread it through the attachment point on your mobile, purse or any zip.

CHARM HOLDER

This can be threaded on a 'European style' charm bracelet to dangle a traditional charm from, or used with cord as a pendant bail for a charm necklace.

DECORATIVE SOLID RING

Unlike a jump ring, this ring doesn't have a gap. It is a secure ring for attaching charms and findings. It can be flat and is often patterned or twisted for added interest.

CHARM RING BLANK

This is an adjustable ring blank with closed loops along the top for attaching beads and charms. The amount of loops can range from 1 to 14 and there are numerous designs available.

EYEPINS AND HEADPINS

These are lengths of wire about 2in (50mm) long with either a small open loop or a pinhead at one end. They are used to connect beads and charms together or onto other components.

BAG CLIP

This is a large trigger clasp that clips onto a bag. The loop at the bottom swivels and charms can be attached directly, or onto a length of chain that is then attached to the loop with a large jump ring.

TRIGGER/LOBSTER CATCHES

CHARM RING BLANK

MOBILE PHONE LARIAT

EYEPIN

CHARM HOLDERS

DECORATIVE SOLID RING

SPLIT RING FOR KEY RING

BAG CLIP

Basic Techniques

THIS SECTION TEACHES YOU A FEW BASIC TECHNIQUES THAT WILL BE USEFUL WHEN MAKING SPECIFIC CHARM PROJECTS IN THIS BOOK, BUT THEY WILL ALSO COME IN HANDY FOR ANY FUTURE CRAFT PROJECTS YOU MAY EMBARK ON.

jump rings

These are available to buy ready-made in various sizes and thicknesses and are often cheaper bought in bulk. However, if you are using them a lot, or require odd sizes for a particular design, it may be easier and cheaper to make your own.

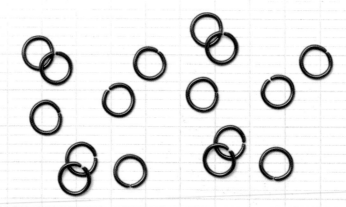

USING JUMP RINGS

It is important to know how to open and close jump rings when you use them to attach items, without destroying their shape.

1 Take two pairs of pliers (flat- or snipe-nose work well) and hold one pair in each hand.

2 Grip both sides of the jump ring, keeping the opening in the centre at the top.

3 Gently move the left-hand pliers away from you and the right-hand pliers towards you. This will open the jump ring while keeping the circular shape intact. To close the jump ring, reverse the technique until the ends meet and are flush against one another.

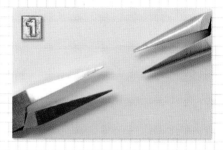
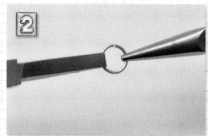
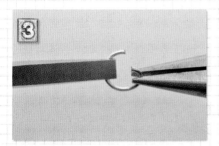

MAKING JUMP RINGS

1 Take a length of round wire in the thickness you require and wrap tightly around multi-sized looping pliers or any suitably sized cylindrical, non-tapered object, to create a neat coil. As you coil the wire, make sure there are no gaps in between each loop.

2 The number of coils made equals the number of jump rings you will produce, so keep wrapping until you have your required amount… or you run out of room!

3 Slide the coil of wire off the object and use side or end cutters to cut the jump rings off one at a time.

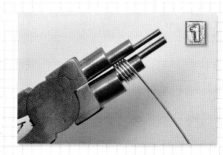
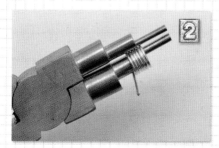

Basic techniques

eyepins and headpins

These are both used as an alternative to jump rings to attach beads, charms or other components to each other. Headpins are a single length of wire (any length) and have a tiny pinhead at one end that acts as a stopper for any beads that are threaded onto the wire. Eyepins are the same, but have a small loop at one end instead of the pinhead. This still secures beads but also allows you to add items onto the loop.

MAKING EYEPINS

An average wire thickness used for making eyepins is 0.8mm (SWG21, AWG 20) but if you have small beads with tiny holes you will need to use thinner wire.

1 Cut a length of wire long enough to thread your beads onto, or work with the wire still on the roll. Using round-nose pliers, hold the wire at the very end.

2 Turn the pliers to form a small closed loop. How far along the pliers you grip the wire will dictate the size of the loop.

3 Flip the loop over on the plier jaw so that the long end of wire is now in between the two jaws. Push the wire back against the jaw without the loop on – this will centre the loop over the remaining wire.

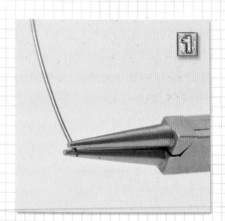

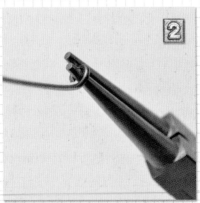

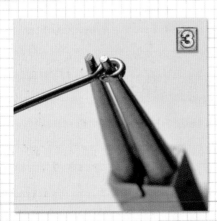

MAKING OPEN EYE LOOPS

This is a loop made in a headpin or eyepin, after a bead has been threaded on. It should be as close to the top of the bead as possible. You can use the loop to attach the bead to another component.

1 Thread a headpin or eyepin through a bead.

2 Bend the length of wire back against the bead to a 90-degree angle. Keep the head or loop of the pin flush with the bead.

3 Take your round-nose pliers and grip the wire at the very top of the bead. (The further towards the tip of the pliers you grip the wire, the smaller the loop will be.) Hold onto the end of the wire with your free hand and wrap it tightly back around the tip of the pliers, all the way around until a full loop is formed.

4 Using side or end cutters, cut the wire at the point where it crosses over itself.

5 Slide the loop onto the round-nose pliers and grip the very end of the cut wire. Bend the wire round and in to meet itself, to finish with a perfect loop.

MAKING WRAPPED LOOPS

This is a loop similar to the open eye loop but instead of cutting off the excess wire after the loop is formed, you wrap it around itself to create a closed loop. This is a secure way to attach beads to your design as once they are wired on they cannot be removed without wire cutters.

1 Thread a bead onto a head or eyepin, making sure it goes all the way down the shaft and that the head of the pin is flush with the bead.

2 Bend the length of wire back against the bead to a 90-degree angle. Keep the head or loop of the pin flush with the bead.

3 Grip the bent wire with your round-nose pliers just beyond the bend. With your other hand, pull the end of the wire back around the tip of the pliers. Go all the way around and make a loop until the wire points in the other direction.

4 Now thread the chain, ear wire or other finding along the wire and into the loop, so that you will be closing the wrapped loop with the item attached.

5 Hold the top of the loop with snipe-nose pliers, and holding onto the end of the wire with your other hand, wrap it around the wire below the loop until it forms a spiral on top of the bead.

6 Using side or end cutters, snip off the remaining wire as close to the end of the spiral as you can. Then, using the tip of the snipe-nose pliers, gently push the cut end of the wire in against the spiral to prevent a sharp edge. If necessary, carefully straighten the loop with your round-nose pliers.

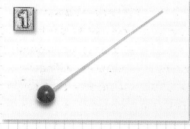

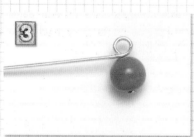

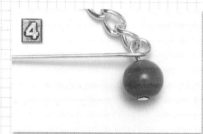

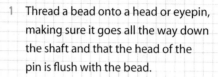

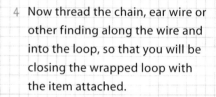

beads, buttons and bows

Used alongside your charms, these inexpensive items will add interesting details to your designs. They are widely available in numerous colours, patterns and sizes but why not create your own for a perfect match?

COVERING BUTTONS WITH FABRIC

Self-cover buttons are available in all haberdashery stores and are so easy to use that it is definitely worth having a go! Make sure you buy the metal buttons that require no tool. These buttons come in various sizes but the technique is always the same.

1 Place the button face down on your fabric, draw a circle ³/₈in (1cm) bigger all the way around the button and cut out the fabric circle.

2 Place the button front face down on the wrong side of the material. Then fold the fabric over the sides of the button and secure by hooking onto the teeth inside the rim. If you are using bulky fabric you should moisten it to help keep the edges smooth.

3 Keep going until all the fabric is secured and the edges are smooth.

4 Place the button back over the loop with the ridge facing down and use your fingers to snap it into place.

5 Now turn the button over and it should be neatly covered and ready to use!

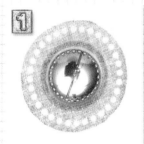

COVERING BEADS WITH FABRIC

A good way to recycle old fabric or use up spare scraps of fabric, covering wooden beads is perfect for creating unique designs to use alongside your charms.

1. Cut your fabric into strips measuring 2³/₄ x 1¹/₄in (7 x 3cm). I have used ³/₄in (2cm) diameter beads so if you use different-sized beads you will have to adjust the sizes of your strips.

2. Hold the bead with your fingers, covering the holes, and squirt a thick line of PVA multi-purpose glue around the whole circumference of your bead.

3. Position your bead in the middle of your fabric strip at one end and roll the fabric around it, making sure the bead holes are visible at each side.

4. Cover the overlapping fabric with more glue and press down all the way along the overlap.

5. Cut small slits into the fabric that extends above one end of your bead to create a fringe effect. Cover the fringe with glue.

6. Fold each individual strip of the fringe in towards the bead hole and neaten by poking something like a pen into the hole after every few strips have been folded down.

7. Once all the strips are folded, use your fingers to smooth any uneven bits and then poke your pen in again to ensure the hole in the bead is still open. Repeat on the other side of the bead and allow to dry.

MAKING A BOW

Learn how to make your own bows so you have the perfect size and colour for your designs. For the Crystal project (see page 104) you need about 8¾in (22cm) of ribbon to make a good-sized bow, but you can change the length of the ribbon according to the size of bow you would like.

1 Find the centre of the ribbon and hold it here.

2 Create a loop on both sides of the centre of the ribbon with tails crossing over each other to create an 'x' shape.

3 Using a needle and black thread, put a stitch through the middle of the bow, making sure you go through the front of the ribbon and the two pieces behind it.

4 Keeping the needle on the thread, wrap the thread around the middle of the bow about six times, pulling it in tightly to create the finished bow appearance.

5 Stitch through the middle of the bow again and tie a secure knot. Use a lighter to seal the ends of the ribbon to prevent fraying. Light the flame and hold each end of the ribbon close enough to it for it to melt slightly.

Basic techniques

Mixed
materials

natasha

Inspired by the Russian doll trend,
this hand-painted wooden charm is
both fashionable and appealing to
children and adults alike.

Everything you will need...

Although designed to accessorize your mobile phone, this charm could also brighten up a purse or small bag.

1. 2 x tiny wooden beads in different colours
2. Silver-coloured eyepin
3. Round plastic flower bead
4. Wooden Russian doll charm
5. Mobile phone attachment

Round-nose pliers

Side cutters

natasha

Assembling natasha

1 Thread one of the wooden beads onto an eyepin followed by the flower bead and then the other wooden bead.

2 Using the pliers, make a loop at the other end of the pin as close to the second bead as possible, then using the side cutters, cut off the excess wire to leave the loop but don't close it (see page 23).

3 Thread the Russian doll charm onto the open loop underneath the bead and close the loop using the pliers.

4 Take the mobile phone attachment and prise open the split ring that is attached to the bottom of it.

5 Thread the split ring through the top loop above the first bead and at the opposite end to the Russian doll charm.

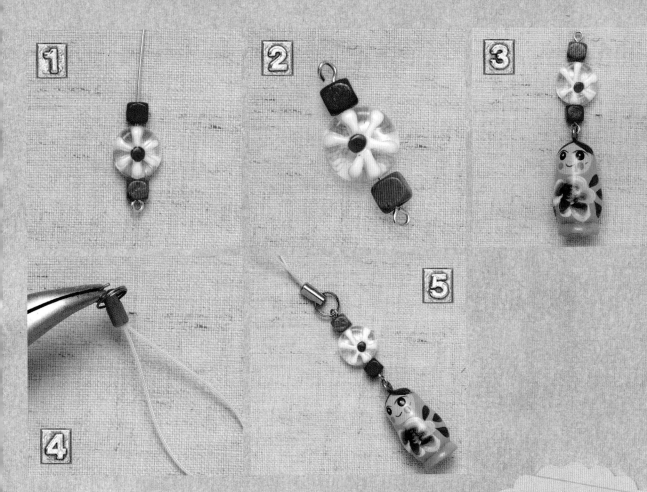

PAINTED WOODEN
CHARMS AND BEADS
ARE AVAILABLE IN
VIBRANT COLOURS AND
PATTERNS - PERFECT
FOR CREATING
FUN DESIGNS!

natasha

cara

There is no need for catches with
this simple, adjustable cord bracelet.

Everything you will need...

Striking glass European charms add a splash
of colour and pretty patterns to this straight-
forward bracelet design.

MAKE A FEW
BRACELETS USING
BRIGHTLY COLOURED
CORDS AND DIFFERENT
CHARMS. HAVE FUN
LAYERING THEM ON
YOUR WRIST!

1 20in (50cm) coloured waxed cord

2 3 x European glass charms

3 Scissors

Tape measure

cara

Assembling cara

1 Measure your desired bracelet length around your wrist, then double it, and add half again. Cut that length of cord. String your charms onto the cord.

2 Loop the cord into a circle. Take the cord that is lying on top and make a fold 5in (12.5cm) from its end so the cord bends back onto itself (this is called the 'working cord'). You should now have three cords side by side.

3 Loop the working cord around to the back, and underneath the other cords.

4 Wrap the working cord around the other cords again and take the end away from the bend, not towards it.

5 Make one more wrap around the cords as before.

6 Take the working cord's end and pass it back through the wrapping, exiting through the initial bend.

7 Hold onto the cords and pull the working cord's end to tighten the knot.

8 Turn the bracelet over and repeat steps 2 to 7 to make a second knot.

9 Trim the cord ends close to the knots. Slide the knots along the cord to open and close the bracelet.

VARY THE DESIGN BY THREADING ON A CHARM HOLDER AND ATTACHING DANGLING CHARMS WITH JUMP RINGS.

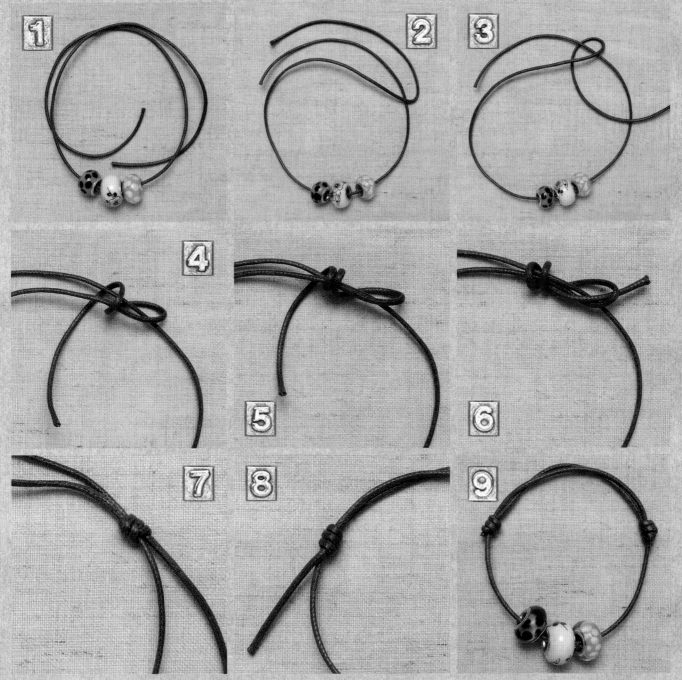

cara

fiesta

Bring out your inner
Carmen Miranda with
these fabulously
fruity statement
earrings!

Everything you will need...

Kitsch plastic charms such as these brightly coloured fruits add an element of fun, retro style to any design. They are perfect for wearing at summer parties!

1 2in (5cm) silver-coloured curb chain (5mm x 3.5mm link size)

2 Pair of silver-coloured earring hooks

3 18 x 5mm silver-coloured jump rings

4 18 x plastic fruit charms:
2 x oranges, 2 x red apples, 2 x purple plums, 2 x green pears, 2 x grapes, 2 x bananas, 2 x pairs of cherries, 4 x leaves

End or side cutters

Flat- or snipe-nose pliers

Assembling fiesta

1 Using the end or side cutters, cut a piece of chain seven links long. Using the pliers, open the loop at the bottom of the earring hook (the same way you open a jump ring – see page 21), thread the end link of the chain onto it and close.

2 Using the pliers, open three of the jump rings and thread them onto the biggest charms – the orange, apple and plum. Attach them to the loop at the bottom of the earring hook.

3 Use another jump ring to attach the green pear to the first link of the chain.

4 Use another jump ring to attach the grapes to the second link of the chain.

5 Attach the banana to the third link, the cherries to the fourth link and a leaf to the fifth link, using a jump ring for each.

6 Use a jump ring to attach the other leaf to the last link of the chain.

7 Repeat all of the steps to create a matching earring.

TO CREATE THIS LOVELY CASCADING SHAPE,
REMEMBER TO ATTACH THE LARGEST CHARMS
AT THE TOP OF THE CHAIN AND THEN
THE OTHERS IN DESCENDING SIZE
ORDER TOWARDS THE BOTTOM.

dreamcatcher

Inspired by the legend that a dreamcatcher
lets only good dreams in, this bracelet
is positively aspirational!

Everything you will need...

This simple plaiting technique can be used with different materials to create either chunky or delicate, colourful or patterned designs. Try leather, waxed cord, ribbon or anything else that takes your fancy.

1 Approx. 39in (1m) brown leather or suede thong

2 2 x silver-coloured ribbon crimps

3 5 x 5mm gold-coloured jump rings

4 Silver-coloured trigger catch

5 7 x 4mm gold-coloured jump rings

6 6 x charms: feather, bells, cross, heart, circular and rectangular tags with your choice of words

Tape measure

Scissors

Flat- or snipe-nose pliers

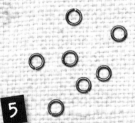

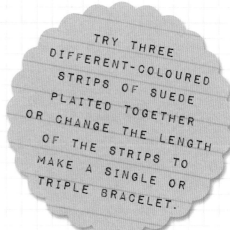

TRY THREE DIFFERENT-COLOURED STRIPS OF SUEDE PLAITED TOGETHER OR CHANGE THE LENGTH OF THE STRIPS TO MAKE A SINGLE OR TRIPLE BRACELET.

Assembling dreamcatcher

1 Wrap the leather once around your wrist, measure this length. Add on another third of the measurement again. For example, for a 6in (15cm) wrist length, add on another 2in (5cm) to equal 8in (20cm). As the bracelet will wrap around the wrist twice, double the final measurement to 16in (40cm) and add ³/₄in (2cm) to allow for the ends of the leather crossing over each other. The final measurement would be 16³/₄in (42.5cm).

2 Cut the leather to your calculated measurement and cut two more equal-length strips. Put the three level ends into the ribbon crimp.

3 Using the pliers, fold the sides over and squeeze tightly to secure the leather strips.

4 Plait the leather, trying to keep the widest part of the leather strip facing upwards so that the bracelet stays flat, not twisted.

5 Plait as far as you can to the end of the leather strips, then if necessary trim the ends so they are level. This is a good point to wrap the bracelet around your wrist to see if you are happy with the length. If not, trim it to the length you prefer. Place the level ends into the second ribbon crimp and secure as before.

6 Using the pliers, open the 5mm jump ring (see page 21) and thread it onto one ribbon crimp. Close the jump ring with the pliers. Open one of the 4mm jump rings and thread it onto the other ribbon crimp then thread the trigger catch onto it. Close the jump ring with the pliers.

7 Thread the six remaining 4mm jump rings onto each of the charms and leave open.

8 Thread each jump ring with a charm attached through one section of the plaited leather bracelet and close. Space the charms evenly around the bracelet, attaching some to the top section of the plait and some to the bottom section.

9 Fold the plait so that it forms a double bracelet.

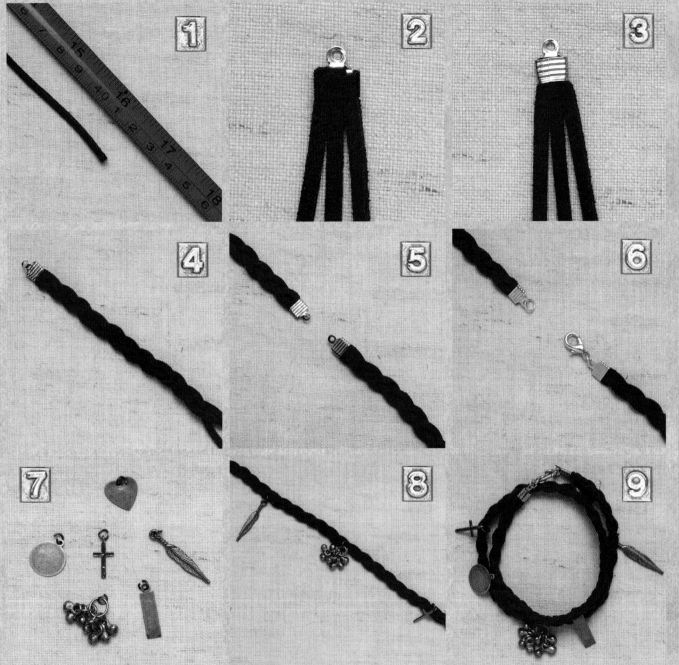

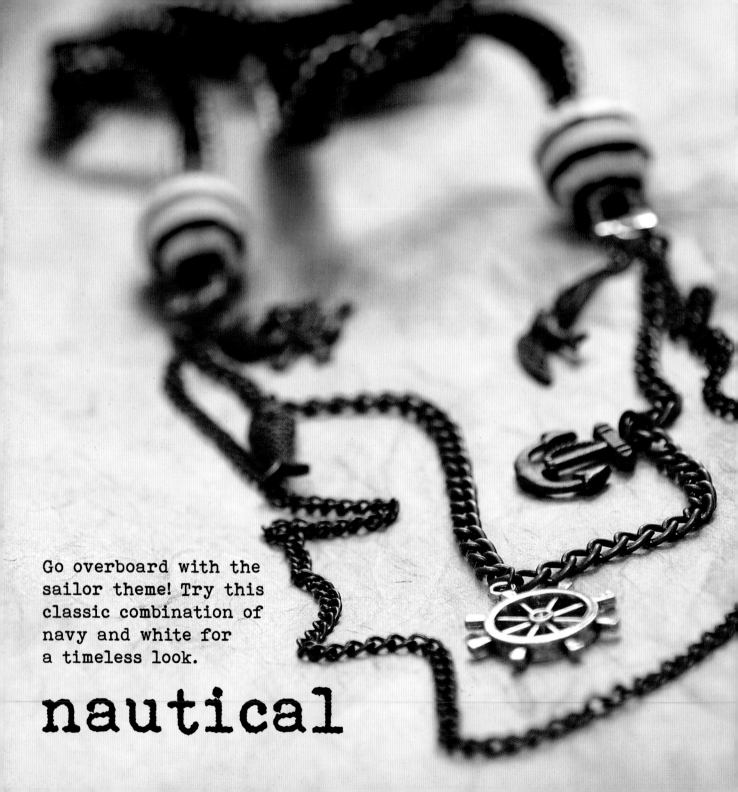

Go overboard with the sailor theme! Try this classic combination of navy and white for a timeless look.

nautical

Everything you will need...

Using ribbon alongside or instead of chain to make necklaces and bracelets is a great way to add a splash of colour and also adjust the lengths depending on how you tie them.

1. 2 x 20mm wooden beads
2. 8in x 3¼in (20cm x 8cm) blue and white stripy fabric
3. 34in (86cm) blue and white ribbon
4. 2 x silver-coloured ribbon crimps
5. 11½in (29cm) gold-coloured heavy curb chain (7mm x 5mm link size)
6. 19¼in (49cm) gold-coloured light curb chain (5mm x 3.5mm link size)
7. 2 x 8mm gold-coloured jump rings
8. 5 x 5mm gold-coloured jump rings
9. 5 x different charms: swallow, skull, anchor, ship's wheel, fish

Scissors

PVA multi-purpose glue

Tape measure

Flat- or snipe-nose pliers

nautical

Assembling nautical

1 Cover your two wooden beads in the fabric (see page 26), making sure that you leave the holes uncovered, and leave to dry.

2 Cut the ribbon into two pieces, both measuring 17in (43cm) long.

3 Put one end of each piece into a ribbon crimp and, using the pliers, squeeze the crimp together tightly to secure the ribbon.

4 Twist the end of the ribbon into a point and thread through the fabric-covered bead until the bead reaches just above the crimp. Repeat on the other ribbon.

5 Using the pliers, open the two 8mm jump rings (see page 21). Thread the end of the heavy chain onto one of the rings and then thread the end of the lighter chain onto the left of it. Repeat with the other ends of the chains. Leave the jump rings open.

6 Thread the jump rings with the chains attached onto the loops on the ribbon crimps and then close the jump rings with the pliers.

7 Use one of the 5mm jump rings to attach the swallow charm to the left side of the 8mm jump ring that the chains are attached to. Then attach the skull charm in the same way to the right-side 8mm jump ring.

8 Using the remaining three 5mm jump rings and counting from the top left, attach the anchor charm to the 18th link of the heavy chain, the ship's wheel charm to the 33rd link and the fish to the 54th link.

9 Wear your necklace by tying the ribbon in a bow at the back of your neck.

USING MULTIPLE CHAINS OF VARYING LENGTHS IN ONE DESIGN WILL HAVE LOADS OF IMPACT AND MAKE AN EYE-CATCHING PIECE OF JEWELLERY.

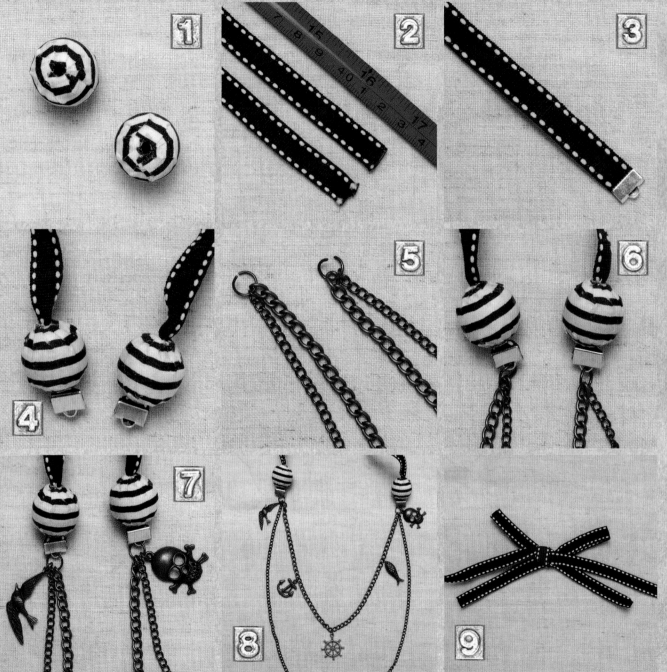

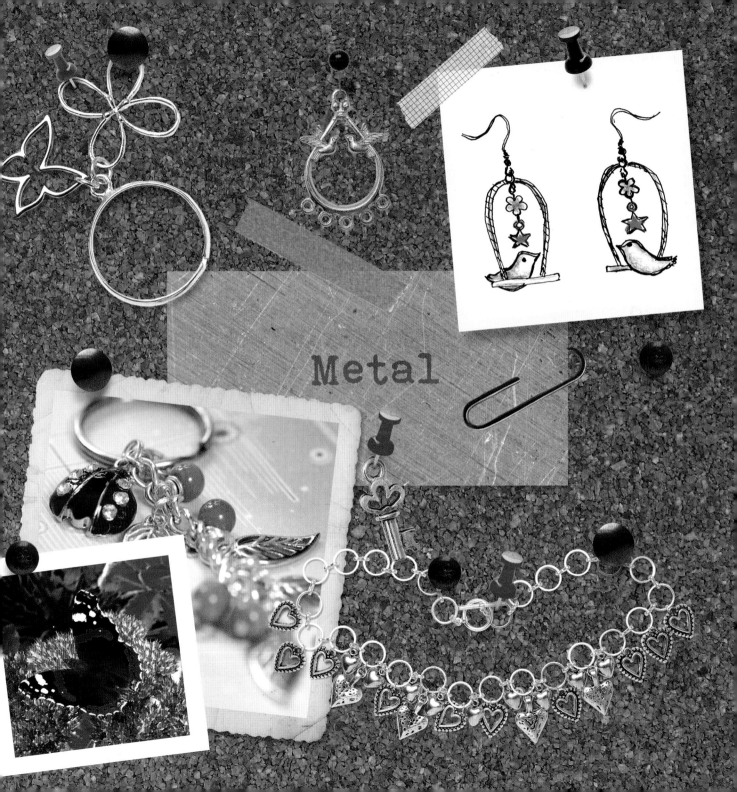

Metal

ladybird

The endearing image of a
ladybird travelling along
a leaf inspired this charming
key ring design.

Everything you will need...

This key ring is intended for everyday use, so split rings are used to attach the charms for added strength and security.

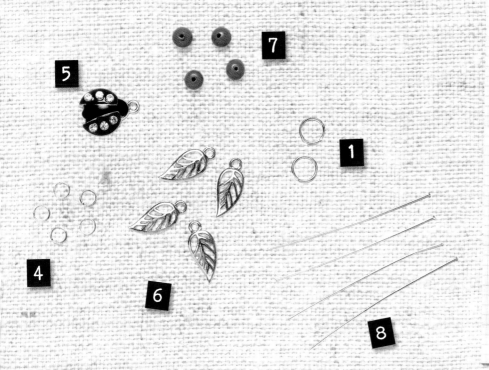

1. 2 x 8mm silver-coloured jump rings
2. 2$\frac{1}{8}$in (5.5cm) silver-coloured heavy curb chain (7mm x 5mm link size)
3. Large, silver-coloured key ring split ring
4. 5 x small silver-coloured split rings
5. Ladybird charm
6. 4 x silver-coloured leaf charms
7. 4 x round green beads
8. 4 x 2in (50mm) silver-coloured headpins

Flat- or snipe-nose pliers

Round-nose pliers

End or side cutters

Small file

Scissors

Assembling ladybird

1 Using the flat- or snipe-nose pliers, open the two jump rings (see page 21) and thread through the end of the chain. Thread onto the large split ring and close.

2 Prise open one of the small split rings and thread the ladybird around it until the ring is completely attached and the charm is hanging freely. Repeat the process with the four leaves and the remaining small split rings.

3 Take the ladybird and again prise open the small split ring. This time thread it onto the left side of the second link from the top of the chain.

4 Take the four leaves and using the split rings on each one, attach one to the right side of the fourth link from the top, one to the left side of the seventh link, one to the right side of the ninth link and one to the bottom link.

5 Thread a green bead onto one of the headpins and, using the round-nose pliers, create a loop (see page 23).

6 Hold the third link of the chain with the flat- or snipe-nose pliers and thread along the long length of the headpin and into the loop you have made.

7 Holding the top of the loop with the pliers, wrap the long end of the wire around itself twice, creating a little spiral on top of the bead (see page 24).

8 Repeat steps 5, 6 and 7 but attach the beads to the sixth, tenth and bottom links of the chain.

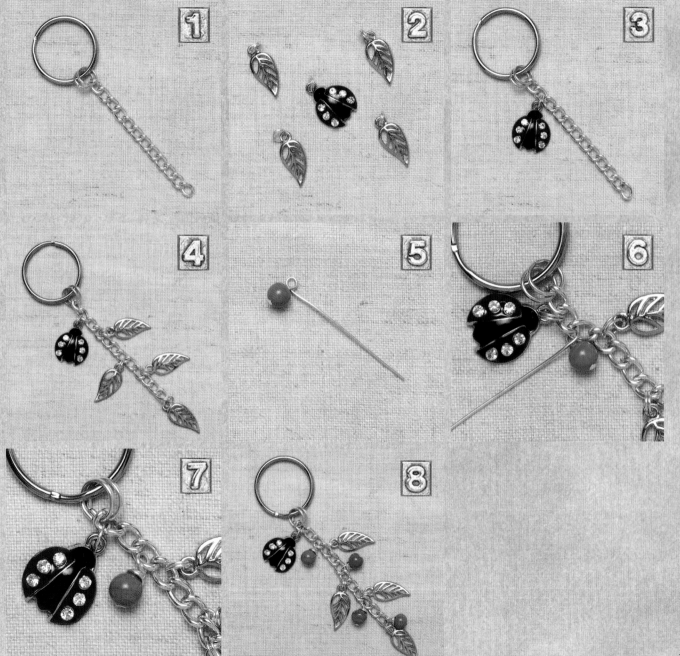

amy

This chunky necklace works
day or evening, adding a
'wow factor' to any outfit.

Everything you will need...

Create this contemporary chain with 'Quick Links'.
They come in various shapes and sizes so you can
create your own, unique designs with ease.

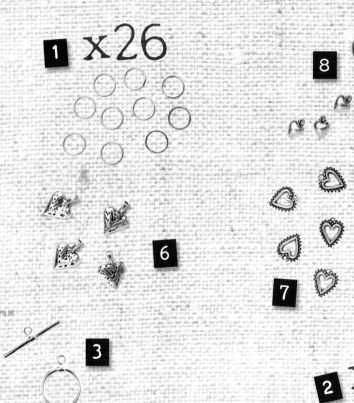

1 x26

8

6

7

3

2 x25

4 x17

5 x14

1. 26 x silver-coloured 'Quick Links' links

2. 25 x silver-coloured 'Quick Links' connectors

3. Silver-coloured T-bar and end loop

4. 17 x 5mm silver-coloured jump rings

5. 14 x 4mm silver-coloured jump rings

6. 4 x large, silver-coloured solid heart charms

7. 10 x silver-coloured open heart charms

8. 9 x silver-coloured small heart charms

Flat- or snipe-nose pliers

Assembling amy

1 Take one 'Quick Links' link and one connector. Place the link in one side of the connector and, using the pliers, squeeze from the top and bottom of that side of the connector to close and secure the link.

2 Take another 'Quick Link', place into the other side of the connector and secure as in step 1.

3 Take another connector and attach to the 'Quick Links' already connected from before. Continue to attach all 26 links and 25 connectors together to create the chain. If you would like the necklace to be longer, just continue to add links until you have the length you want.

4 Using the pliers, open one of the 5mm jump rings (see page 21) and thread onto the loop of the T-bar. Attach the jump ring to the last link on one end of the chain. Then add another 5mm jump ring to make sure that the T-bar is securely attached given the weight of the finished necklace. Repeat on the other end of the chain, attaching the catch with two more jump rings.

5 Lay the necklace flat and count 13 links down one side from the catch to find the middle connector.

6 Take the four large solid heart charms and attach and close a 5mm jump ring to each. Then count two links up from the middle connector of the chain and attach a heart using one of the 4mm jump rings through the 5mm jump ring already attached. Count two links from there and attach another heart. Repeat these two steps on the opposite side of the chain.

7 Take five open heart charms and starting from the middle connector attach one charm with a 4mm jump ring to each empty link. Repeat as a mirror image on the other side of the chain.

8 Take one small heart and use a 5mm jump ring to attach around the middle connector. Attach four small hearts with 5mm jump rings to the next four connectors alongside one side of the chain. Repeat as a mirror image on the opposite side of the chain.

WHEN THE CHAIN IS LAID FLAT, IMAGINE THE LINKS HAVE TWO HALVES – ONE FACING INSIDE AND ONE FACING OUTSIDE. ALWAYS ATTACH THE CHARM TO THE OUTSIDE OF THE LINK SO ALL THE CHARMS WILL HANG EQUALLY.

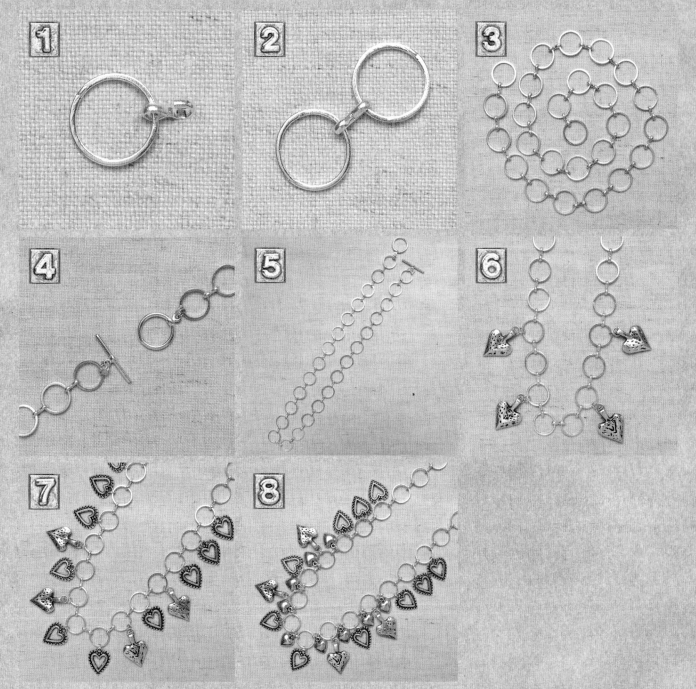

flutter

The gentle flutter of a butterfly's wings is reflected in the movement of these suspended charms.

Everything you will need...

Fine, open wire charms keep this pretty charm ring lightweight, delicate and contemporary.

1. Silver-coloured, adjustable, single-loop ring blank
2. 2 x 4mm silver-coloured jump rings
3. Gold-coloured wire butterfly charm
4. Silver-coloured wire flower charm

Flat- or snipe-nose pliers

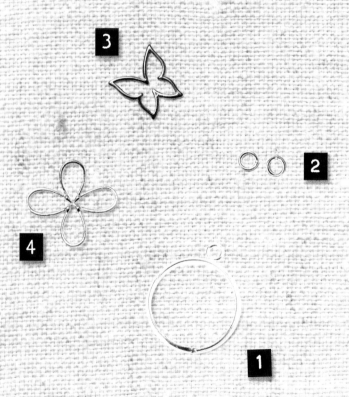

3

2

4

1

FOR A MORE DRAMATIC EFFECT, ADD MORE CHARMS ONTO THE LOOP AND WIRE ON SOME BEADS OR PEARLS USING HEADPINS (SEE PAGES 22-3).

Assembling flutter

1 Take the ring blank and stretch it until you reach the size required to fit on your finger.

2 Using the pliers, open one of the jump rings (see page 21) and thread the butterfly charm onto it.

3 Attach the jump ring and butterfly charm to the loop on top of the ring blank.

4 Open the other jump ring and thread the flower charm onto it.

5 Attach the jump ring and flower charm to the loop on top of the ring blank, next to the butterfly charm.

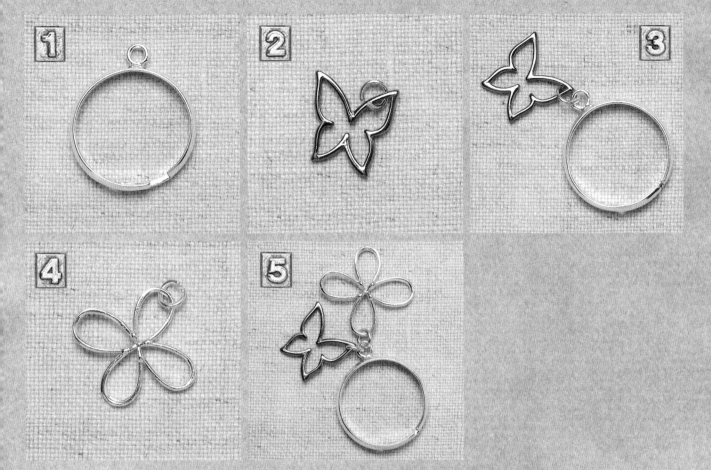

owl

Add a bit of sparkle to your books
with this unusual bookmark.

Everything you will need...

Imagine the beautiful scene of a wise owl sitting under the twinkling night sky outside your window as you read…

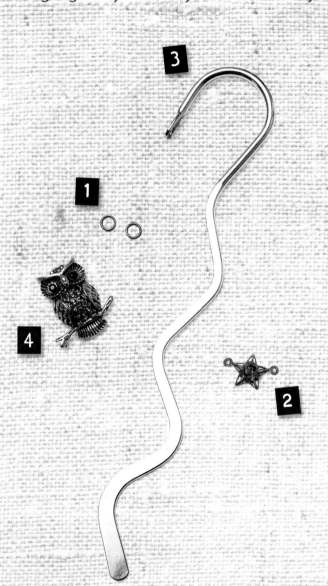

1. 2 x 5mm gold-coloured jump rings
2. Gold-coloured star charm connector
3. Large, silver-coloured zigzag bookmark blank
4. Crystal-encrusted owl charm

Flat- or snipe-nose pliers

METAL BOOKMARKS ARE AVAILABLE WITH SMOOTH, DECORATIVE, STRAIGHT OR ZIGZAG SHANKS AND HAVE A LARGE LOOP AT THE END WHERE CHARMS CAN BE ATTACHED.

Assembling owl

1 Using the pliers, open one of the 5mm jump rings (see page 21) and thread it onto one loop of the star charm connector.

2 Attach the jump ring and star connector to the large loop on the end of the bookmark.

3 Open the other 5mm jump ring and attach it to the other loop of the star charm connector. Leave the jump ring open.

4 Thread the owl charm onto the open jump ring from the previous step.

5 Close the jump ring and your sparkly bookmark is ready to use!

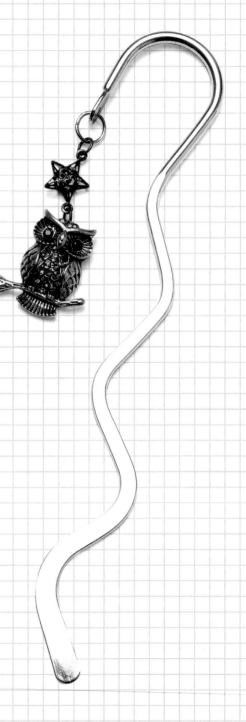

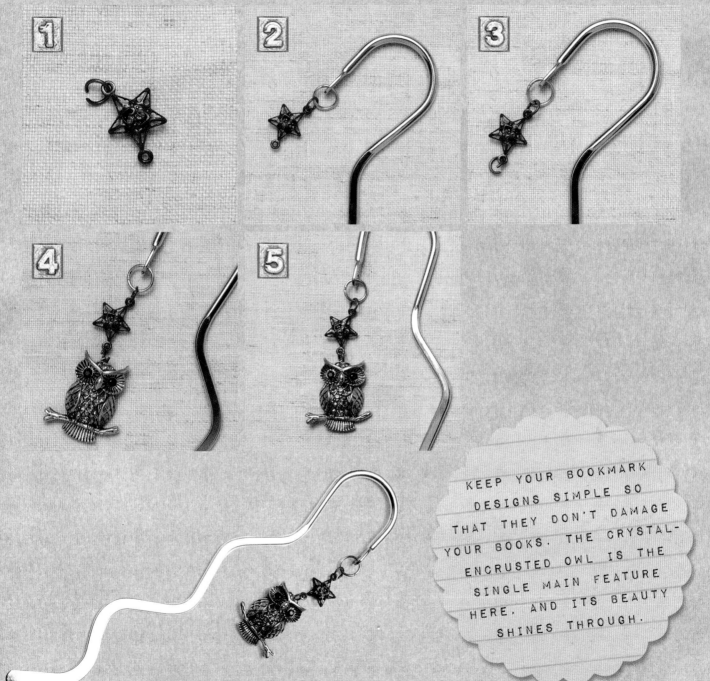

KEEP YOUR BOOKMARK DESIGNS SIMPLE SO THAT THEY DON'T DAMAGE YOUR BOOKS. THE CRYSTAL-ENCRUSTED OWL IS THE SINGLE MAIN FEATURE HERE, AND ITS BEAUTY SHINES THROUGH.

owl

canary

These delightful bird-
on-a-perch charms will
look stunning with
a little black dress and
add style to casual jeans
and a T-shirt.

Everything you will need...

The clever design of these bird charms allows you to add extra charms within them. Swarovski crystal beads have been used here to add sparkle.

1. 2 x silver-coloured earring hooks
2. 2 x silver-coloured bird charms
3. 2 x silver-coloured eyepins
4. 2 x Swarovski crystal flower beads
5. 2 x tiny, gold-coloured star charms

Flat- or snipe-nose pliers

Round-nose pliers

Side cutters

Assembling canary

1 Using the flat- or snipe-nose pliers, open the loop at the bottom of the earring hook (the same way you open a jump ring – see page 21) and thread through the top loop of the bird charm.

2 Take an eyepin and thread on the Swarovski flower bead to the end of the pin. Using the pliers, bend the wire as close to the top of the bead as possible at a 90-degree angle to the bead, with the loop of the eyepin on its side (see page 23).

3 Holding onto the existing loop with the flat- or snipe-nose pliers, use the round-nose pliers to create another loop in the pin, facing the opposite direction to the existing loop. Snip off the excess wire using the side cutters but do not close the loop.

4 Thread the star charm onto the open loop and close the loop using the flat- or snipe-nose pliers.

5 Open the other loop above the bead and thread onto the solid loop inside the bird charm.

6 Now repeat step 1 with the matching earring but this time turn the bird charm around to face the opposite direction. Repeat steps 2 to 5.

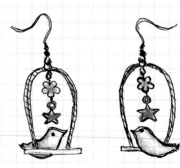

EARRINGS ALWAYS
LOOK BEST WHEN THEY
ARE A MIRROR IMAGE
OF EACH OTHER
BECAUSE THEY BALANCE
AND COMPLEMENT
THE FACE.

vintage and found

button

Fun, colourful and
fashionable... brighten
up any handbag with
this unique design.

Everything you will need...

Buttons come in so many different colours, shapes and sizes that the possibilities for this design are endless!

1	2 x large metal self-cover buttons
2	2 x small metal self-cover buttons
3	Scraps of fabric
4	2³⁄₄in (7cm) silver-coloured heavy curb chain (7mm x 5mm link size)
5	2 x 8mm silver-coloured jump rings
6	Silver-coloured bag clip
7	9 x 5mm silver-coloured jump rings
8	6 x 7mm silver coloured jump rings
9	Orange flower button
10	Sparkly flower button
11	3 x different-coloured/patterned round buttons
12	Red heart button
	Flat- or snipe-nose pliers

1

2

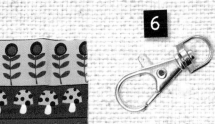

5

4

6

7

8

3

9

11

12

10

button

Assembling button

1 Cover the two large buttons and two small buttons with fabric (see page 25).

2 Using the pliers, open the two 8mm jump rings (see page 21) and thread them onto one end of the chain. Attach the jump rings to the loop at the bottom of the bag clip.

3 Thread one of the 5mm jump rings through one of the large buttons and attach it to the first link of the chain. Then take the other large button and attach it with another 5mm jump ring to the second link of the chain. Close the loops using the pliers.

4 Take the two small buttons and thread a 5mm jump ring through each. Then attach one to the first link of the chain (where the large one is already attached) and the other one to the sixth link of the chain.

5 Take the orange flower button and attach it to the sixth link of the chain using one of the 7mm jump rings.

6 With the five remaining buttons, thread another 7mm jump ring through one hole in each button and close. Then thread a 5mm jump ring through the 7mm jump ring for each button. Leave the second jump ring open.

7 Attach the pink spotty button to the eighth chain link, the purple button to the ninth chain link and the green button to the tenth link.

8 Lastly, attach the flower button to the twelfth link and the heart button to the last link in the chain.

TRY VINTAGE BUTTONS WITH ANTIQUE GOLD-COLOURED CHAIN AND JUMP RINGS FOR A DIFFERENT LOOK!

TRY TO THINK OF EACH CHAIN LINK AS HAVING TWO HALVES (LEFT AND RIGHT). ADD THE BUTTONS RANDOMLY TO EACH SIDE ALONG THE CHAIN.

roxy

Rock your world with these
fun plectrum earrings.

Everything you will need...

Plectrums are available in different thicknesses, ranging from thin to extra heavy; for these earrings it is best to choose the thin variety.

1 2 x green plectrums

2 2 x yellow plectrums

3 2 x orange plectrums

4 8¾in (22cm) silver-coloured 2mm trace chain

5 6 x 5mm silver-coloured jump rings

6 Pair of silver-coloured earring studs with loop fitting

Block of wood

Nail

Hammer

End or side cutters

Flat- or snipe-nose pliers

Assembling roxy

1 Ensure you are working on a solid, stable surface such as a block of wood. Place a plectrum on the wood. Position the nail about ¹/₈in (3mm) from the top of the plectrum in the centre. Tap the nail with the hammer approximately three times until the nail has punctured the plectrum and made a small hole. Repeat this step with all six plectrums.

2 Cut two pieces of chain to 2¹/₈in (5.5cm), cut another two pieces to 1³/₈in (3.5cm) and cut another two pieces of chain to ³/₄in (2cm), using the end or side cutters.

3 Using the pliers, open the 5mm jump rings (see page 21) and thread through the holes in the plectrums.

4 Attach a green plectrum to the end of one of the 2¹/₈in (5.5cm) chains. Attach an orange plectrum to the end of one of the 1³/₈in (3.5cm) chains. Attach a yellow plectrum to one of the ³/₄in (2cm) chains.

5 Take a stud with loop fitting and thread the ³/₄in (2cm) chain with yellow plectrum onto the loop. Then thread the 1³/₈in (3.5cm) chain with orange plectrum onto the loop and finally thread the 2¹/₈in (5.5cm) chain with green plectrum onto the loop. It is important to put the chains on in this order so that the plectrums hang correctly.

6 Close the loop on the stud with the pliers.

7 Repeat steps 5, 6 and 7 to make a matching earring.

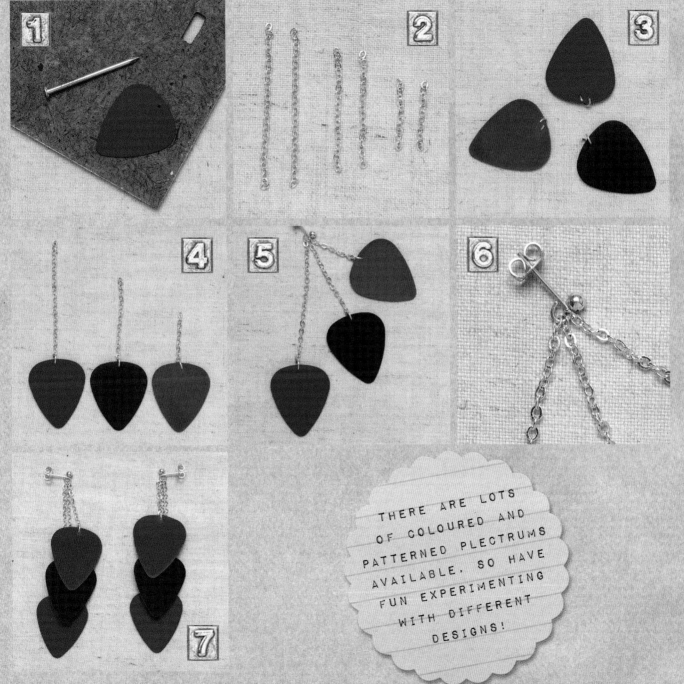

THERE ARE LOTS
OF COLOURED AND
PATTERNED PLECTRUMS
AVAILABLE, SO HAVE
FUN EXPERIMENTING
WITH DIFFERENT
DESIGNS!

roxy

pearl

Make something from nothing by recycling
a long-forgotten broken pearl necklace and
turning it into a unique bracelet.

Everything you will need...

Here, a simple design has been chosen to display one beautiful charm, but you could add more charm holders every few pearls to create a pretty multi-charm bracelet.

1 Approx. 20in (50cm) clear thin elastic

2 Old pearl necklace or bracelet

3 Silver-coloured charm holder

4 5mm silver-coloured jump ring

5 Starfish charm

Scissors

Superglue

Flat- or snipe-nose pliers

Assembling pearl

1 To decide on the exact length of elastic you will need, wrap it around your wrist fairly loosely and leave a bit extra so tying a knot in the end will be easy. Cut this length – don't worry, you can trim off any excess at the end.

2 Unthread your pearls from the old necklace or bracelet.

3 Holding one end of the elastic to stop the pearls from sliding off, thread the pearls onto it until most of the elastic is covered (apart from the excess you have left for the knot).

4 Next, thread the charm holder onto the end after the pearls. Wrap the bracelet around your wrist to check the size. If too large, remove some pearls, or if too small, add some more!

5 Tie a tight double knot with the two ends of elastic and put a drop of glue on it to secure the knot. Trim the excess elastic.

6 Using the pliers, open the jump ring (see page 21) and thread onto the starfish charm.

7 Attach the starfish charm to the charm holder.

TRY THIS DESIGN WITH REAL SHELLS
TO CREATE AN AUTHENTIC BEACH STYLE!

ALWAYS CHECK
THAT THE HOLES
IN ANY BEADS YOU
FIND ARE LARGE
ENOUGH FOR THE
ELASTIC TO SLIDE
THROUGH EASILY.

pearl

robyn

Update your favourite
bag with this quirky
designer bag charm.

Everything you will need...

The beauty of this bird charm is that it is double-sided, so it can flip over and still look great!

1. Dark brown leather offcut
2. Scrap of green felt
3. Scrap of patterned fabric
4. 2⅛in (5.5cm) blue and white ribbon
5. Silver-coloured bag clip
6. 2 x tiny pink buttons
7. 2 x small feathers
8. 2 x small, silver-coloured ribbon crimps
9. 3⅛in (8cm) heavy curb chain (7mm x 5mm link size)
10. 7mm silver-coloured jump ring
11. 2 x tiny bell charms (1 silver-coloured, 1 gold-coloured)
12. 2 x 5mm silver-coloured jump rings

x2

Scissors

PVA multi-purpose glue

Flat- or snipe-nose pliers

Tape measure

robyn

Assembling robyn

1 Draw and cut out two bird shapes from leather – a front and back, approx. 4in (10cm) in length. Cut out two wings from felt approx. 1½in (4cm) in length and two smaller wings from patterned fabric to fit inside the felt wings.

2 Thread the ribbon through the loop at the bottom of the bag clip so that the ends are level.

3 Glue the two bird shapes together and trap the ribbon ends in between them halfway along the top of the bird. Allow to dry before continuing.

4 Glue the felt wing onto the bird and the patterned smaller wing on top of the felt. Also glue the tiny button onto the head as an eye. Repeat on the reverse of the bird. Allow to dry before continuing.

5 Place the quill of one feather in a small ribbon crimp and using the pliers, squash each side of the crimp down so it is tightly shut. Repeat with the second feather.

6 Using the pliers, open the 7mm jump ring (see page 21) and thread onto one end of the chain. Attach the jump ring to the loop at the bottom of the bag clip.

7 Thread a tiny bell charm and one of the feathers onto one of the 5mm jump rings and attach to the last link of the chain.

8 Thread the other bell and feather onto the other 5mm jump ring and attach to the third link from the bottom of the chain.

BUY OFFCUTS OF LEATHER AND FABRICS AT FABRIC OR DEPARTMENT STORES TO HELP YOU KEEP COSTS DOWN AND AVOID WASTAGE. OR USE UP ANY SCRAPS YOU MAY HAVE AT HOME!

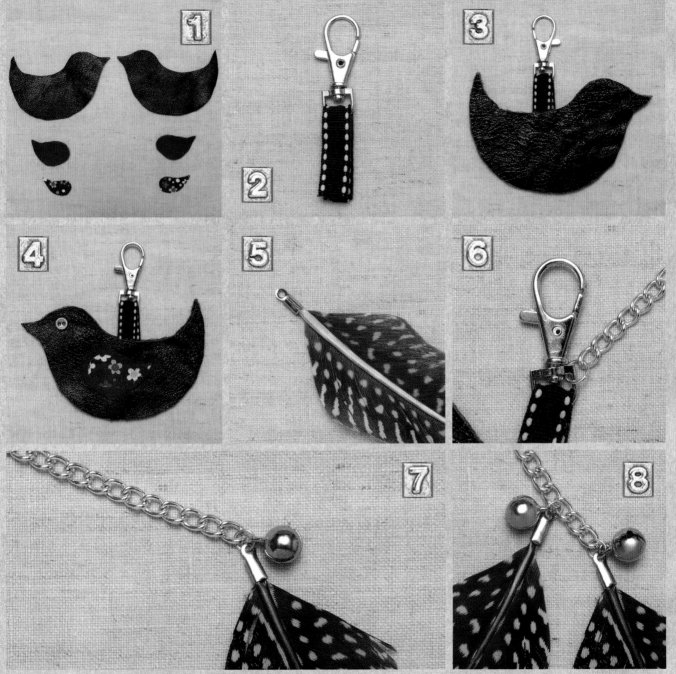

robyn

sweetheart

These quirky earrings send messages of love and affection using classic love-heart sweet charms.

Everything you will need...

Using real candy necklace beads is fun, but plastic love-heart charms are also cheap and easily available. You can change the amount you use or the colours of the beads as often as you like!

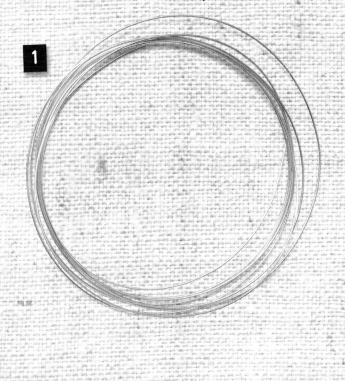

1. 20in (50cm) 0.8mm (SWG 21, AWG 20) silver-coloured round wire

2. 12 x candy necklace sweets

3. 2 x 5mm silver-coloured jump rings

4. 2 x love-heart plastic charms

End cutters

Round-nose pliers

Flat- or snipe-nose pliers

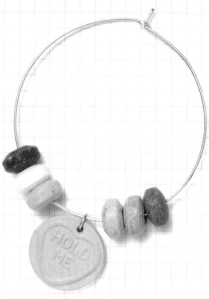

Assembling sweetheart

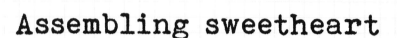

1 Make the earring hoops by coiling the wire twice around a cylindrical object, the size of which will determine the size of your hoops. I have used a pepper grinder to make these large hoops (1³/₄in [4.5cm] inside diameter).

2 Use your end cutters to snip through the wire and separate the hoops.

3 Using round-nose pliers, grip the end of the wire on one side of the hoop and turn to form a small loop.

4 Using flat- or snipe-nose pliers, bend the other end of the hoop approximately 90 degrees away from the hoop to fit through the small loop and secure the hoop. Gently re-shape the hoop with your fingers to ensure it is round.

5 Thread three different-coloured sweets onto the hoop.

6 Using the pliers, open one of the 5mm jump rings (see page 21) and thread it through the love-heart charm. Close the jump ring.

7 Thread the love-heart charm onto the hoop behind the sweets.

8 Thread another three different-coloured sweets onto the hoop after the love-heart charm.

9 Repeat steps 5 to 8 after making the second hoop to create the matching earring.

IF YOU'RE USING REAL SWEETS, COAT THEM IN A THIN LAYER OF CLEAR VARNISH TO ENSURE THEY LAST.

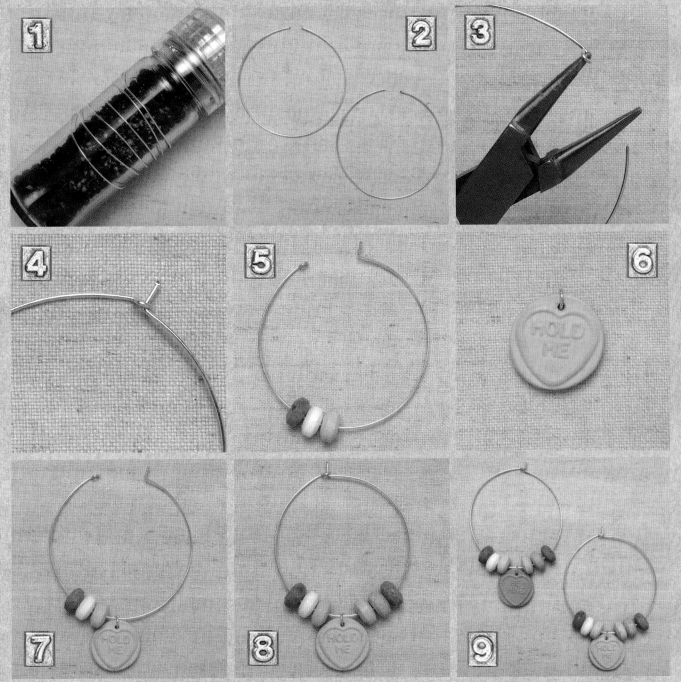

ANNA

Storyboard

polly

Create your own personalized bracelet with charms that symbolize your personality, experiences and aspirations!

Everything you will need...

Each charm is attached to a trigger clasp that can easily be added onto, or removed from, any chain, in any order, at any time. So now you can change your jewellery, as your life changes!

1. Approx. 20in (50cm) silver-coloured fancy curb chain (9mm x 5mm large link size, 5mm x 3mm tiny link size)
2. 10 x 4mm silver-coloured jump rings
3. Silver-coloured T-bar and loop
4. 8 x silver-coloured trigger catches
5. 8 x charms of your choice to personalize your bracelet

String

Tape measure

End or side cutters

Flat- or snipe-nose pliers

Wire snips

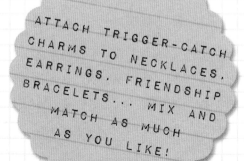

Assembling polly

1 Wrap a piece of string loosely around your wrist to find the length that you would like your bracelet to be. Measure the string and cut your chain to ½in (13mm) shorter than the string, using the end or side cutters.

2 Using the pliers, open one of the jump rings (see page 21) and thread the end catch onto it and then attach to one end of the chain.

3 Open another jump ring and thread the T-bar onto it and then attach to the other end of the chain.

4 Open another jump ring, thread a trigger catch onto it and then thread a charm on afterwards. Close the jump ring with the pliers. Repeat this until all of your charms have a trigger catch attached.

5 Lay the bracelet flat. Count three links in from the end catch and clip a charm onto the third link. Repeat this at the other end of the chain by the T-bar.

6 Count four links along from the first charm and attach the next charm to the fourth link. Repeat this along the bracelet until all charms are attached.

ATTACH TRIGGER-CATCH CHARMS TO NECKLACES, EARRINGS, FRIENDSHIP BRACELETS... MIX AND MATCH AS MUCH AS YOU LIKE!

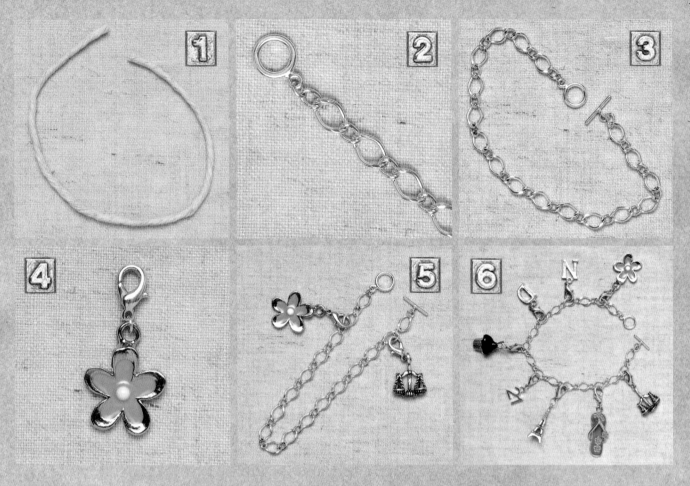

IF YOU HAVE MORE CHARMS, OR WISH TO ADD MORE AT A LATER DATE, YOU CAN REARRANGE THE CHARMS TO HAVE FEWER LINKS BETWEEN THEM OR EVEN ATTACH ONE TO EACH LINK.

clover

These charms are believed to have a positive influence over the fortunes of the wearer, bringing them good luck.

Everything you will need...

Various symbols inspire good fortune, love, health, wealth, happiness… Choose your combination and keep your fingers crossed!

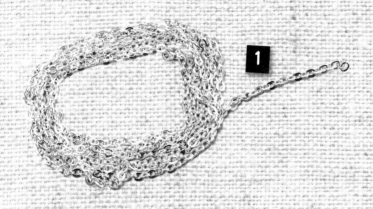

1. Approx. 16¼in (41cm) silver-coloured 2mm trace chain

2. Silver-coloured bail

3. Silver-coloured solid ring

4. 6 x 5mm silver-coloured jump rings

5. 3 x different charms: horseshoe, cloverleaf, wishbone charm

6. Silver-coloured trigger catch

Tape measure

Side cutters

Flat- or snipe-nose pliers

Assembling clover

1 Using the side cutters, cut the chain to your desired length – 16¼in (41cm) is an average length.

2 Open the bail using the pliers.

3 Put the solid ring onto the bail and close using the pliers.

4 Thread the chain through the bail.

5 Open and thread one of the jump rings onto the wishbone charm, and then close (see page 21). Then open another jump ring and thread through the previous jump ring. Because the loop on the wishbone charm is facing the wrong way for the charm to face forwards, two jump rings must be used.

6 Attach the wishbone to the solid ring by the top jump ring and close.

7 Use another jump ring to attach the cloverleaf to the left of the wishbone on the solid ring and then repeat with the horseshoe charm but attach to the right of the wishbone.

8 Open and attach another jump ring at one end of the chain and, using the remaining jump ring, attach a trigger catch to the other end of the chain.

A BAIL MAKES IT POSSIBLE FOR MANY OBJECTS TO BE TRANSFORMED INTO A PENDANT WITHOUT SOLDERING OR DRILLING. IT OPENS AT THE BACK TO THREAD THE CENTREPIECE ON AND THEN FOLDS BACK. IT CAN THEN BE SLID ONTO A CHAIN.

crystal

Wear your heart on your sleeve and show a loved one that they hold the key to your heart.

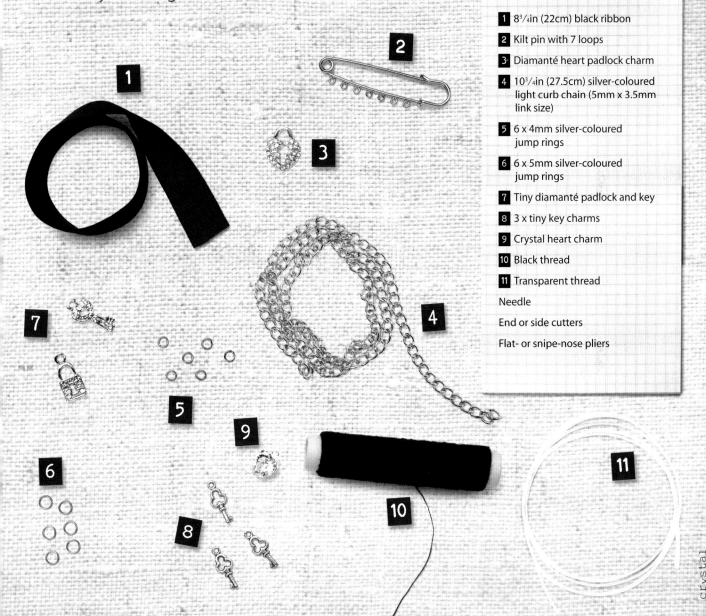

Everything you will need...

Sparkle and shine in style by using diamanté and crystal charms in your designs.

1. 8³/₄in (22cm) black ribbon
2. Kilt pin with 7 loops
3. Diamanté heart padlock charm
4. 10³/₄in (27.5cm) silver-coloured light curb chain (5mm x 3.5mm link size)
5. 6 x 4mm silver-coloured jump rings
6. 6 x 5mm silver-coloured jump rings
7. Tiny diamanté padlock and key
8. 3 x tiny key charms
9. Crystal heart charm
10. Black thread
11. Transparent thread

Needle

End or side cutters

Flat- or snipe-nose pliers

crystal

Assembling crystal

1 Make a bow (see page 27). Place the bow over the large loop in the kilt pin at the opposite end to the opening.

2 Place the diamanté padlock over the front centre of the bow and using transparent thread, sew from the back of the bow through the kilt-pin loop and through the middle of the padlock.

3 Loop over the top of the padlock and around the back, coming back through the loop, and repeat until the charm and bow are securely attached to the kilt pin.

4 Repeat the sewing from step 3 but this time loop the thread around the bottom of the padlock and bottom of the loop. When secure, stitch through the ribbon and tie a knot to secure the thread and trim the excess.

5 Using the end or side cutters, cut a piece of chain to $4\frac{1}{4}$in (11cm), another piece to $2\frac{1}{2}$in (6.5cm), another piece to $2\frac{3}{8}$in (6cm) and the last piece to $1\frac{1}{2}$in (4cm).

6 Attach two of the 5mm jump rings to each end of the $4\frac{1}{4}$in (11cm) chain (see page 21) and then attach one end to the first loop and one end to the last loop on the kilt pin. Then, again using 5mm jump rings, attach one end of the $2\frac{1}{2}$in (6.5cm) chain to the second loop from the left on the kilt pin and one end to the last loop on the right.

7 Use a 5mm jump ring to attach one end of the $2\frac{3}{8}$in (6cm) chain to the first loop on the left. Then use a 5mm jump ring to attach one end of the $1\frac{1}{2}$in (4cm) chain to the jump ring at the top of the $2\frac{3}{8}$in (6cm) chain.

8 Use 4mm jump rings to attach the diamanté key to the loose end of the $2\frac{3}{8}$in (6cm) chain, and the diamanté padlock to the loose end of the $1\frac{1}{2}$in (4cm) chain.

9 Use three 4mm jump rings to attach tiny keys to the sixth, eleventh and sixteenth links, counting from the top right side, of the longer looped chain. Use the remaining 4mm jump ring to attach the crystal heart to the tenth link, counting from the top left side, of the shorter looped chain.

TO VARY THE DESIGN, USE A KILT PIN WITH FEWER LOOPS ATTACHED ALONG THE BOTTOM.

alice

The much-loved story of *Alice in Wonderland* is filled with magical, instantly recognizable characters that make beautiful and fun charms.

Everything you will need...

Using antique gold-coloured chain, findings and charms creates a vintage look that fits perfectly with this quirky necklace.

1 Antique gold-coloured eyepin

2 Large, plastic, red rose bead

3 35¾in (91cm) antique gold-coloured light curb chain (5mm x 3.5mm link size)

4 2 x 7mm antique gold-coloured jump rings

5 5 x 4mm antique gold-coloured jump rings

6 6 x different charms: 'drink me' bottle, clock, 'Alice' heart, teacup, toadstool, teapot

Round-nose pliers

Side cutters

Flat- or snipe-nose pliers

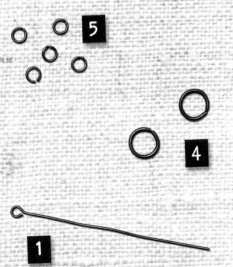

alice

Assembling alice

1 Thread the eyepin through the rose bead and, using round-nose pliers, make an open eye loop on the other side of the bead (see page 23).

2 Using the side cutters, cut a piece of chain 28in (71cm) long and attach each end of the chain to the loops of the rose bead.

3 Cut another piece of chain to 4¼in (11cm) and another piece to 3½in (9cm). Using the flat- or snipe-nose pliers, open one of the 7mm jump rings (see page 21) and thread on the chains – the shorter chain first so it is on the left.

4 Measure 3½in (9cm) down from the rose bead and attach the jump ring and chains through a link in the main chain.

5 Thread the other 7mm jump ring through the loop on the 'drink me' bottle charm and close around the main chain next to the jump ring from step 4. This means the bottle charm is free to move along the chain up to the rose bead.

6 Thread one of the 4mm jump rings onto the clock charm, and then attach it to the fourth link from the top of the 4¼in (11cm) chain. Take another 4mm jump ring and use it to attach the 'Alice' charm to the thirteenth link up from the bottom of the same chain.

7 Attach the teacup charm to the bottom link of the 4¼in (11cm) chain with another 4mm jump ring.

8 Now on the 3½in (9cm) chain, attach the toadstool charm with a 4mm jump ring to the twelfth link up from the bottom of the chain. Finally, attach the teapot charm to the bottom link of the same chain with the last 4mm jump ring.

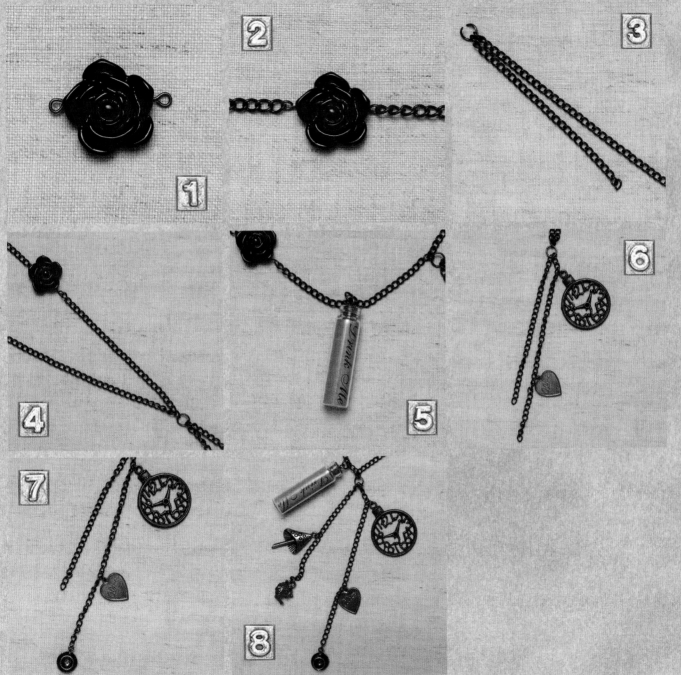

anna Make guests feel special with these personalized wine-glass charms.

Everything you will need...

A thoughtful addition to any party, these charms will make your guests feel welcome and can serve as stylish place settings at a dinner table.

1. 6in (15cm) 0.8mm (SWG 21, AWG 20) silver-coloured round wire to make 1 charm
2. 3 x coloured beads
3. Alphabet beads of your choice
4. 4mm silver-coloured jump ring
5. Charm of your choice
6. Flat- or snipe-nose pliers

End cutters

Round-nose pliers

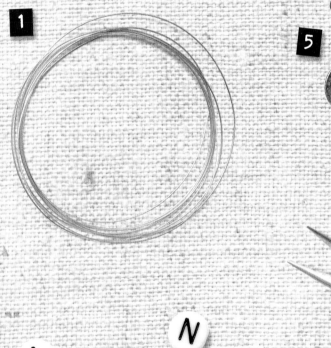

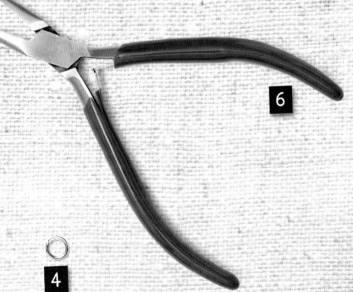

Assembling anna

1 Make the loops by wrapping the wire around a cylindrical object of the correct size, such as a nail-varnish bottle, until you have the desired amount of loops for the number of charms you wish to make.

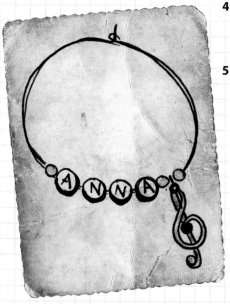

2 Use your end cutters to snip the wire and separate the loops.

3 Using the round-nose pliers, make a small loop at one end of the wire.

4 Thread a coloured bead onto the ring, then the letter beads and two more coloured beads.

5 Using the flat- or snipe-nose pliers, bend the other end of the wire 90 degrees upwards to fit into the small loop and secure the ring.

6 Using the pliers, open the jump ring (see page 21) and thread on the charm. Close the jump ring and then attach it to the ring in between the two coloured beads.

7 Put the charm around the base of a glass and secure.

USE SEASONAL
CHARMS TO MARK
DIFFERENT OCCASIONS
SUCH AS CHRISTMAS,
BIRTHDAYS OR
EVEN SUMMER
BARBECUES.

anna

resources

UK

The Bead Shop
Afflecks Palace
52 Church St
City Centre
Manchester
M4 1PW
Tel: +44 (0)161 833 9950
www.the-beadshop.co.uk

Bead Time
14 Castle Street
Kingston upon Thames
KT1 1SS
Tel: +44 (0)20 3166 0046
www.beadtime.co.uk

Beads Direct Ltd
10 Duke Street
Loughborough
Leicestershire
LE11 1ED
Tel: +44 (0)1509 218028
www.beadsdirect.co.uk

Beadworks Bead Shop
21a Tower Street
Covent Garden
London
WC2H 9NS
Tel: +44 (0)207 240 0931
www.beadworks.co.uk

Big Bead Boutique
12 Dyke Rd
Brighton
BN1 3FE
Tel: +44 (0)1273 383983
www.bigbeadboutique.co.uk

Bijoux Beads
2 Abbey Street
Bath
BA1 1NN
Tel: +44 (0)1225 482024
www.bijouxbeads.co.uk

The Birmingham Bead Shop
The Custard Factory
Gibb Street
Digbeth
Birmingham
B9 4AA
Tel: +44 (0)121 2511413
www.thebirminghambeadshop.
co.uk

The Brighton Bead Shop
21 Sydney Street
Brighton
East Sussex
BN1 4EN
Tel: +44 (0)1273 675077
www.beadsunlimited.co.uk

Cookson Precious Metals Ltd
59–83 Vittoria Street
Birmingham
B1 3NZ
Tel: +44 (0)845 100 1122
www.cooksongold.com

Fabric Land
76 Western Road
Brighton
East Sussex
BN1 2HA
Tel: +44 (0)1273 822257
www.fabricland.co.uk

Hatton Garden London
49 Hatton Garden
London
EC1N 8YS
Tel: +44 (0)845 100 1122
http://www.hatton-garden.net/
preciousmet.html

Hobbycraft
Stores Nationwide
Tel: +44 (0)1202 596100
www.hobbycraft.co.uk

JillyBeads Ltd
1 Anstable Road
Morecambe
LA4 6TG
Tel: +44 (0)1524 412728
www.jillybeads.co.uk

Kerrie Berrie
10 Sydney Street
Brighton
East Sussex
BN1 4EN
Tel: +44 (0)1273 624285
www.kerrieberrie.co.uk

My Vintage Charms
www.myvintagecharms.com

USA

Artbeads.com
11901 137th Ave. Ct. KPN
Gig Harbor
Washington
98329
Tel: 1.253.857.3433
www.artbeads.com

Beaded Impressions, Inc.
7340 S Alton Way
Ste #11-J
Centennial
Colorado
80112
Tel: 1.800.532.8480
www.abeadstore.com

Charm Factory
5921 Office Blvd NE
Albuquerque NM 87109
Tel: 1.866.867.5266
www.charmfactory.com

Fire Mountain Gems
Customer Service
1 Fire Mountain Way
Grants Pass
Oregon
97526-2373
Tel: 1.800.355.2137
www.firemountaingems.com

Shipwreck Beads
8560 Commerce Place Drive
Northeast
Lacey
Washington
98516
Tel: 1.800.950.4232
www.shipwreckbeads.com

CANADA

Great Big Bead Store
2441 Lakeshore Blvd.
West
Oakville
Ontario
L6L 5V5
www.greatbigbeadstore.com

GENERAL

www.etsy.com

about the author

Sophie Robertson is a jewellery designer/maker currently living and working in Brighton in the south-east of England. Sophie graduated from Loughborough University School of Art and Design in 2002 with a BA (Hons) in Silversmithing and Jewellery Design and has worked for various established designers over the last ten years. She designs and makes her own jewellery collections and has created many beautiful bespoke commission pieces for clients.

Sophie has a passion for working with metals but her inspiration also comes from experimenting with diverse materials and techniques, continuing to highlight the limitless possibilites of jewellery design. Her love of art and craft has also inspired her to share her knowledge and skills. She has worked with adults and children of all ages and abilities in many different settings, teaching jewellery design and making but also a wide range of fun, craft-based, creative projects.

index

Project names are given in italics

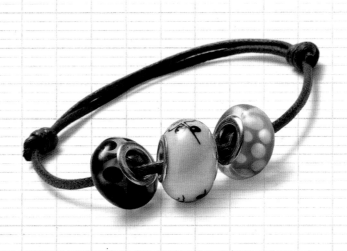

To order a book, or to request
a catalogue, contact:

GMC Publications Ltd
Castle Place,
166 High Street,
Lewes,
East Sussex,
BN7 1XU
United Kingdom

Tel: +44 (0)1273 488005

www.gmcbooks.com